A Diller, A Dollar

by Annalisa McMorrow
illustrated by Marilynn G. Barr

Publisher: Roberta Suid
Design & Production: Scott McMorrow
Educational Consultant: Shirley Ross
Cover Design: David Hale
Cover Art: Mike Artell

Also in this series:
Ladybug, Ladybug (MM 2015), *Twinkle, Twinkle* (MM 2016),
Rub-a-Dub-Dub (MM 2017), *Pussycat, Pussycat* (MM 2036),
Daffy-Down-Dilly (MM 2037), *Rain, Rain, Go Away!* (MM 2038),
Snips & Snails (MM 2096), *Sticks & Stones* (MM 2097),
The Wheels on the Bus (MM 2098)

Contents

Introduction

A Diller, a Dollar is composed of five chapters, each a complete unit dedicated to a specific type of money. This resource has a cross-curricular approach that helps children develop a hands-on understanding of currency while strengthening language skills, such as speaking and listening. Children will learn to relate to money in a personal way: learning through games, observations, literature links, math activities, songs, and art.

Let's Read features a popular children's book, such as *Bunny Money* by Rosemary Wells, and is accompanied by a detailed plot description. **Let's Talk** helps children link the featured book with familiar feelings, thoughts, or happenings in their own lives. For example, in the Quarters chapter, the "Let's Talk" discussion focuses on a time when children had a difficult time waiting for something. This page also includes a pattern that can be duplicated and used as a bookmark.

Let's Learn is filled with facts about each type of currency. For example, the building on the back of modern pennies is the Lincoln Memorial. Choose facts that you think will interest the children. Read a fact a day during the unit. Or write down different facts and post them on bulletin boards around the room.

The **Let's Create** activities in each chapter encourage children to use their imaginations while honing small motor skills. The children will make pennies featuring their own self-portraits, create purple purses, and more.

Children make a hands-on learning connection in the **Let's Find Out** activities. These projects focus on exploration, leading children through moments of discovery as they count coins, sort shapes, and much more.

Let's Play suggests a new game to interest children in the featured monetary unit. **Let's Eat** offers suggestions for snacks that tie into the chapter's theme. Songs sung to a familiar tune are featured in the **Let's Sing** section. Children can learn the new lyrics and perform them for parents or each other. Duplicate the songs and send them home with the children to share with their families.

Informative Pattern Pages complete each chapter. These patterns can be duplicated and used for bulletin board displays, reduced for cubby labels or name tags, or used for desk labeling. (Children can color the patterns using crayons or markers.) Some of the patterns in this book would be perfect to use for decorations during Presidents' Day, Independence Day, Lincoln's Birthday, or George Washington's Birthday.

At the end of the book, you'll find a Storybook Resources section filled with additional fiction picture books and storybooks, plus a Nonfiction Resources section suggesting factual and photographic books.

All About Money

Only people who are historically significant, and no longer living, can have their pictures on American money. Most of the people featured on American money were presidents. However, Benjamin Franklin, who is on the 100-dollar bill, was not a president. He was a printer, inventor, postmaster, and statesman. Salmon P. Chase, featured on the 10,000-dollar bill was the twenty-fifth secretary of the treasury. Alexander Hamilton was the first secretary of the treasury. He is featured on the ten-dollar bill. Susan B. Anthony, who is on a dollar coin, was influential in winning women's right to vote.

Some other countries feature characters or people who aren't political on their money. For instance, a bill in France features a picture of The Little Prince, a beloved character from a French storybook.

American bills are made from a secret mixture of black and green dyes. All American bills look the same color green. Other countries aren't limited to one color for their bills. Some use many different colors to help prevent their bills from being counterfeited.

Before there were bills and coins, people used a variety of unusual items in place of money. These include small feathers, shells, salt, cocoa, large stones with holes in the center, and bundles of tobacco leaves.

Pennies

Introduction

• Let's Read:
Alexander, Who Used to Be Rich Last Sunday by Judith Viorst, illustrated by Ray Cruz (Atheneum, 1978). Alexander and his two brothers all like money. Still, Alexander has nothing but bus tokens at the start of this book, but he remembers a week ago when he had a whole dollar. Although his mother told him he should save his dollar toward the walkie-talkie he wants, throughout the week, he spends his pennies, nickels, and dimes on various items.

• Let's Talk:
Although Alexander tries to save his money, he is tempted by too many things he wants to buy, such as gum, a candle, a used teddy bear, and an hour with his friend's snake. Have the children try to put themselves in Alexander's position. Would they have been tempted by the various items, like Alexander was? Or would they have been able to save their dollar?

    This is also an appropriate time to discuss the value of money. This story was written in 1978, when a dollar could buy more than it can now. Ask the children to think of things that they might be able to buy with a dollar. The list probably won't be as long as Alexander's.

• Let's Learn:
The man on the penny is Abraham Lincoln. He is one of our former presidents. On the backside of modern pennies is the Lincoln Memorial. Older pennies, which are sometimes called "wheatbacks," have a different design on their flip side. All United States coins have two sayings stamped on them: In God We Trust and E Pluribus Unum (Latin for "out of many, one").

Pennies

Let's Create: Beautiful Banks

Old-fashioned piggy banks had to be broken to remove the money inside. These banks can be used for years.

What You Need:

Cans with plastic lids (such as coffee cans), construction paper, glue, crayons or markers, decorative items (buttons, sequins, rickrack, lace or fabric scraps, pictures from magazines), knife (for adult use only)

What You Do:

1. Cut a slit (for coins) in each lid.
2. Give each child a can to decorate up to the rim, not over the lid. The children can decorate their cans to look like animals or objects, or simply cover the cans with pictures and other decorative items.
3. Help the children put the lids on the cans.
4. The children can take their banks home for coin storage. When they want to get their money, they need only pop open the lids.

Options:

• Use individual-size juice containers with plastic lids or round oatmeal boxes instead of cans.
• Have the children do penny rubbings before this activity. They can cover their banks with the rubbings of the pennies.
• Teach the children the saying, "A penny saved is a penny earned."

Pennies

Let's Create: Personal Pennies
The children will enjoy putting their own pictures on pennies.

What You Need:
Pennies, construction paper, scissors, crayons or markers

What You Do:
1. Cut the construction paper into circles. Make one circle for each child.
2. Pass around the pennies for the children to study. Ask if anyone knows whose picture is on the penny. If the children do not know, tell them that the person on the penny is Abraham Lincoln. Then ask if any of the children know the name of the building on the back of the pennies. If nobody knows, explain that this building is the Lincoln Memorial. (Older pennies have a picture of wheat on the back.)
3. Give each child a construction paper circle. Explain that the children will be creating new pennies. These will have their self-portraits on them. Provide crayons or markers for the children to use to draw their self-portraits.
4. The children can draw pictures of their houses on the backs of the pennies.
5. Have each child share his or her new penny with the class.
6. Post the Personal Pennies on a bulletin board using a hinge of tape at the top so that viewers can lift the pennies to see the houses on the backs.

Abraham Lincoln Facts to Share:
Lincoln was born in Kentucky. He lived from 1809 until 1865. He was our sixteenth president, and he was in office from 1861 to 1865. A picture of Lincoln is also on the $5 bill. The Lincoln Memorial was built in his honor. It is in West Potomac Park, Washington, D.C.

Option:
• Ask parents to send in photographs of their children. Explain that these photos will be used in an art project.

Pennies

Let's Create: Lucky Pennies

Many people consider it good luck to find a penny. The children will make their own lucky pennies in this activity.

What You Need:

"Find a Penny" rhyme (below), "I'm a Penny!" pattern (p. 19), scissors, hole punch, yarn, crayons or markers, glue, decorative items (sequins, buttons, lace or fabric scraps)

What You Do:

1. Duplicate a copy of the "I'm a Penny!" pattern for each child and punch a hole in the top of each pattern.
2. Teach the children the "Find a Penny" rhyme. Ask if any of the children have ever found a penny. Let the children share any stories they have.
3. Give each child a penny pattern. They can glue decorations in a circle around the penny.
4. Help the children thread a piece of yarn through the hole in their penny patterns.
5. Hang the pennies in the classroom, or let the children take their lucky pennies home to hang in their rooms.

Option:

• For "show and tell," ask the children to bring in any lucky item they have.

Find a Penny

Find a penny,
Pick it up,
And all day you'll have good luck.
Find a penny,
Let it lie,
And good luck will pass you by.

Pennies

Let's Find Out: Counting Coins

This activity introduces the children to the concepts of different coins equalling different amounts of money.

What You Need:

"I'm a Penny!" (p. 19), "I'm a Nickel!" (p. 31), "I'm a Dime!" (p. 32), scissors, copper-colored paper, gray paper

What You Do:

1. Duplicate the "I'm a Penny!" pattern onto copper-colored paper. Make ten copies and cut them out.
2. Duplicate two copies of the "I'm a Nickel!" pattern and one copy of the "I'm a Dime!" pattern onto gray paper and cut them out.
3. Have the children sit in a circle on the floor.
4. Spread the ten penny patterns on the floor. Have the children count them aloud. Explain that each penny equals one cent.
5. Bring out the two nickel patterns. Explain that each nickel is worth as much as five pennies. Have the children count out five pennies for each nickel.
6. Bring out the dime pattern. Explain that a dime is worth as much as ten pennies. Ask the children to think of different ways that their paper coins could be put together to equal the dime. (They could line up the ten pennies, or the two nickels, or five pennies and one nickel.)
7. Let the children continue to play and count with the paper coins. Store the coins in a large manilla envelope for later counting activities.

Option:

• Duplicate 100 copies of the penny pattern and let the children practice counting to 100 by ones.

Pennies

Let's Find Out: Shape Sorting

This activity reinforces the children's recognition of shapes.

What You Need:
Shape Patterns (p. 13), colored construction paper, scissors, large envelope (for storage)

What You Do:
1. Duplicate the Shape Patterns onto different colors of construction paper and cut them out.
2. Have the children name the shape of a penny (round, or a circle).
3. Explain that the children will be sorting objects by their different shapes. Pick up one of the shapes and say, "This is a square." Let the children take turns picking up the shapes and placing them in the appropriate piles.
4. Make sure each of the children has a chance to sort.

Note:
The children can sort the shapes by color, making piles of all the green shapes regardless of whether the shapes are circles, triangles, rectangles, and so on.

Option:
• Store the shapes in an envelope. Let the children practice shape sorting during free time.

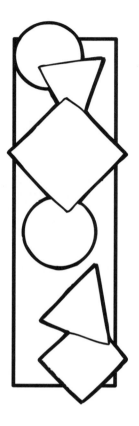

Shape Patterns

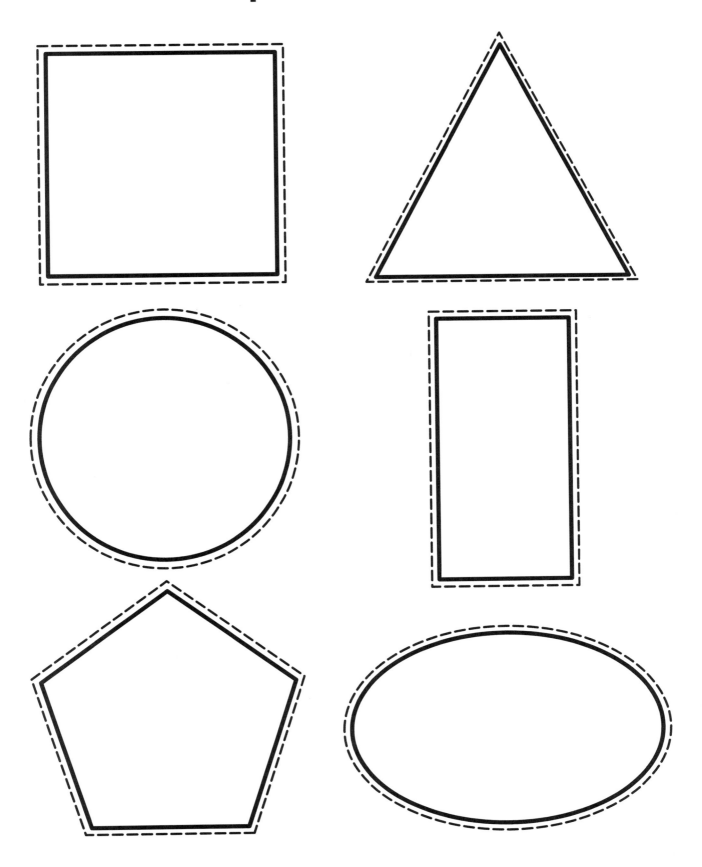

Pennies

Let's Play: Coincentration
This game is played like "Concentration."

What You Need:
Coincentration Cards (p. 15), markers or crayons, scissors, clear contact paper or laminator (optional)

What You Do:
1. Duplicate the cards twice, color, and cut out. Laminate or cover with clear contact paper, if desired. Cut out again leaving a thin laminate border to prevent peeling.
2. Demonstrate how to play "Coincentration." The children turn all the cards face down. The first child turns two cards over at a time. If the cards match, the child keeps them and takes another turn. If the cards do not match, the child turns them back over and another child takes a turn.

Option:
• Use the Coincentration Cards to reinforce recognition of different coins. Some children may never have seen a Susan B. Anthony dollar or a half-dollar.

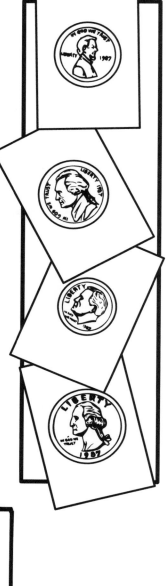

Coincentration Cards

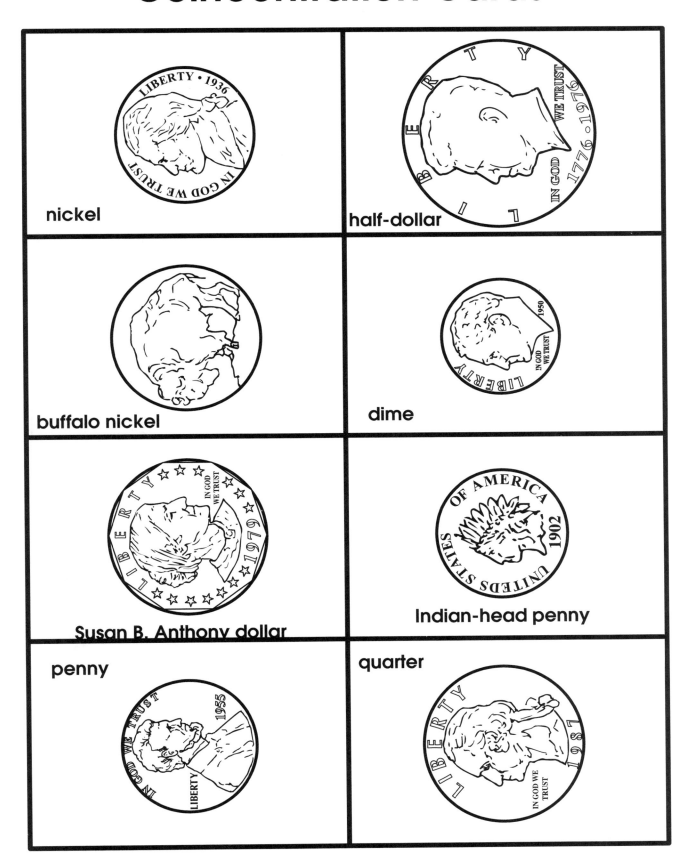

nickel

half-dollar

buffalo nickel

dime

Susan B. Anthony dollar

Indian-head penny

penny

quarter

Pennies

Let's Eat: Penny-Shaped Snacks

What You Need:
Carrots, cucumbers, cream cheese, round crackers, knife (for adult use only)

What You Do:
1. Cut the carrots and cucumbers into thin, round slices.
2. Serve the round crackers with cream cheese and the vegetable slices.
3. Have the children name the shape of their snacks. Ask them how the shape is similar to a penny. (Both are round.)

Options:
• Serve other round snacks, such as cookies or hard-boiled eggs cut in circles.
• Serve slices of pie. Give each child a penny to use to "pay" for the pie. Teach the children the Mother Goose rhyme "Simple Simon" (p. 18) before serving this snack.
• Serve hot cross buns. Teach the children the Mother Goose rhyme "Hot Cross Buns" (p. 18) before serving this snack.

Book Link:
• "The Slow-Eater-Tiny-Bite-Taker Cure" is a chapter in the book *Mrs. Piggle-Wiggle* by Betty MacDonald, illustrated by Hilary Knight (Lippincott, 1947). In it, Mrs. Piggle-Wiggle cures a little boy's habit of eating tiny bites by having his mother serve his food on penny-sized dishes.

Pennies

Let's Sing: Penny Songs

I'm a Little Penny
(to the tune of "I'm a Little Teapot")

I'm a little penny,
Colored brown.
I'm not square,
My shape is round.
Shake me up inside your piggy bank,
I make noise like clink-clank-clank.

Oh, My Darling, Piggy Bank
(to the tune of "Clementine")

Oh, my darling,
Oh, my darling,
Oh, my darling, piggy bank.
I will put in all my pennies,
And I'll listen to them clank.

P Is for Penny
(to the tune of "C Is for Cookie")

P is for penny,
And penny starts with "p."
P is for penny,
And penny starts with "p."
P is for penny,
And penny starts with "p."
Oh, penny, penny, penny starts with "p."

Pennies

Let's Learn: Mother Goose Rhymes

Simple Simon
Simple Simon met a pieman
Going to the fair.
Said Simple Simon to the pieman,
"Let me taste your wares."
Said the pieman to Simple Simon,
"Show me first your penny."
Said Simple Simon to the pieman,
"Indeed, I have not any."

Hot Cross Buns
Hot cross buns.
Hot cross buns.
One-a-penny,
Two-a-penny,
Hot cross buns.
If you have no daughters,
Give them to your sons.
Hot cross buns.
Hot cross buns.

I'll Sing You a Song
I'll sing you a song,
Though not very long,
Yet I think it as pretty as any;

Put your hand in your purse,
You'll never be worse,
And give the poor singer a penny.

Lucy Locket
Lucy Locket lost her pocket,
Kitty Fisher found it;
Not a penny was there in it,
Only ribbon round it.

One-a-penny,
Two-a-penny,
Hot cross buns.

"I'm a Penny!"

Nickels & Dimes

Introduction

• Let's Read:
Dollars and Cents for Harriet by Betsy and Giulio Maestro (Crown, 1988).
In this "money concept" book, Harriet the elephant needs five dollars to buy a kite. She has 100 pennies, but she works to earn nickels, dimes, quarters, and half-dollars until she reaches her goal. The children can count along with Harriet as she earns money.

• Let's Talk:
Harriet does a wide variety of chores. Have the children share any chores they do at home. They might clear the table, rake leaves, make their beds, and so on. Give each child a chance to share how he or she helps out at home.

Harriet earns 20 nickels and 10 dimes. This book is the perfect introduction to a wide variety of counting and simple math activities. Have the children count along with you as you read the story. If your school has any fund raisers, use this book to get the children involved. Harriet earns money for a kite by doing a variety of chores for her neighbors. Your students might be able to help rake leaves or wash cars, like Harriet does.

• Let's Learn:
The man on the front of the nickel is Thomas Jefferson. His picture is also on the two-dollar bill. He was our third president and is known for writing the Declaration of Independence. He lived from 1743 to 1826. He was also an inventor and an architect. On the back of the nickel is a picture of Monticello. This was Thomas Jefferson's home. It is in Charlottesville, Virginia.

Nickels & Dimes

Let's Create: Old-Fashioned Trading

In the story *Dollars and Cents for Harriet*, Harriet trades her skills for money.

What You Need:
Playdough, clay, or other craft materials

What You Do:
1. Explain to the children that before people had money to spend, they traded items or services. For instance, a hunter might trade meat with a carpenter for building services.
2. Provide clay or playdough for the children to use to make sculptures or pots.
3. Once the crafts dry, let the children trade with each other.

Note:
You can make the trades temporary—just for one day, and then have the children trade back.

Option:
• The children can also make drawings, paintings, or other crafts to trade.

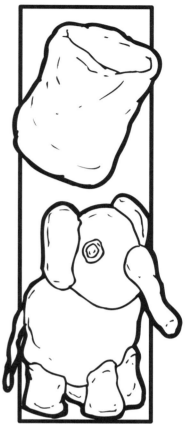

Nickels & Dimes

Let's Create: Buffalo Nickels

Before Thomas Jefferson was on the nickel, these coins featured pictures of buffalo.

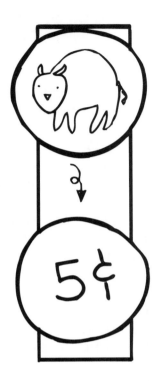

What You Need:
Books about buffalos, jar lids, construction paper, markers or crayons, scissors

What You Do:
1. Show the children pictures of buffalos. Discuss the fact that throughout history, coins have featured pictures of different people or objects. Explain that early nickels featured pictures of buffalo.
2. Have the children trace the jar lids onto construction paper to make circles. The children can then cut out the circles.
3. The children can draw pictures of buffalo on one side of the circles. On the other side, they can draw the numeral five and a cents sign.
4. Post the buffalo nickels on a "Beautiful Buffalo" bulletin board.

Option:
• Have the children choose other animals to feature on coins. Each child can draw a different animal and then introduce his or her new coin to the class.

Nickels & Dimes

Let's Find Out: Fives and Tens

What You Need:
"I'm a Nickel!" pattern (p. 31), "I'm a Dime!" pattern (p. 32),
counters, scissors, large envelopes (for storage)

What You Do:
1. Duplicate the "I'm a Nickel!" and "I'm a Dime!" patterns
and cut them out.
2. Hold up the "I'm a Nickel!" picture and ask the children how
many cents a nickel is worth.
3. Have the children work in small groups to make piles with
five counters per pile.
4. As a class count to 100 by fives.
5. Hold up the "I'm a Dime!" picture and ask the children how
many cents a dime is worth.
6. Have the children think of different things that equal the
number ten: they have ten fingers and ten toes. A dime is
worth ten pennies and a dollar is worth ten dimes.
7. Have the children work in small groups to make piles with
ten counters per pile.
8. As a class, count to 100 by tens.
9. Store the patterns in large envelopes to use in other
counting activities.

Option:
• Make sets of 20 of the "I'm a Nickel!" patterns and ten of the
"I'm a Dime!" patterns for the children to use in this activity.
Children can work in groups to count by fives and tens.

Nickels & Dimes

Let's Find Out: Dime Rhymes

This fun language activity will have children looking for rhymes everywhere.

What You Need:

"I'm a Dime!" pattern (p. 32), chalk, chalkboard, paper, crayons or markers

What You Do:

1. Duplicate the "I'm a Dime!" pattern and post it in the room.
2. Have the children look at the pattern. Then ask them to think of as many words as they can that rhyme with the word "dime." Allow near rhymes, such as vine, if the children have difficulty thinking of rhyming words. (Use the list below if needed.)
3. Write down the words as children come up with them.
4. Have each child choose a word from the list to illustrate.
5. Bind the finished pages in a "Rhymes with Dime" picture book.

Words That Rhyme with Dime:

Chime, crime, grime, lime, mime, rhyme, prime, thyme, time

Near-Rhymes for Dime:

Dine, fine, line, mine, pine, sign, vine, whine, wine

Option:

• During the year, have the children search for rhymes for other words.

Nickels & Dimes

Let's Play: Put It in the Bank

This is a game about saving. The children will each be trying to get to the bank to deposit their money.

What You Need:
Markers & Spinner (p. 26), Game Board pattern (p. 27), crayons or markers, clear contact paper (or laminating machine), scissors, hole punch, brad

What You Do:
1. Duplicate the Game Board pattern, color, and cover with contact paper. (Or use a laminating machine.)
2. Duplicate the Markers & Spinner, cut out, color, cover with clear contact paper, and cut out again. (Leave a thin laminate border to help prevent peeling.)
3. Punch a hole in the center of the spinner, and attach the arrow using the brad.
4. Explain the game. Three children may play at a time. The players are each little elephants trying to get to the bank first to deposit their money. The first child to land at the spot marked "finish" is the winner.

Markers & Spinner

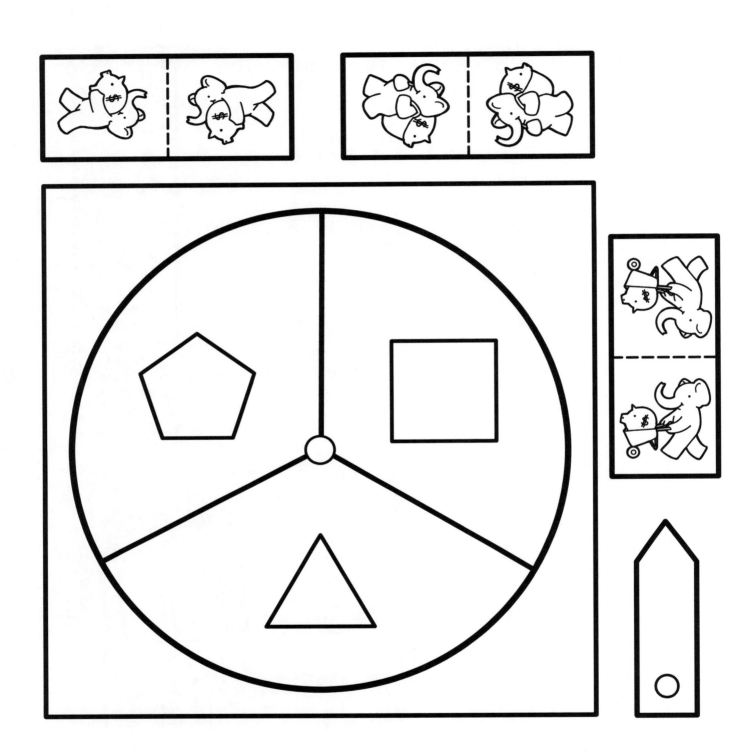

Game Board

27

Nickels & Dimes

Let's Eat: Pickle Snacks

What You Need:
An assortment of pickles (sweet, dill, pickle relish served on crackers, tiny French pickles called "cornichon")

What You Do:
1. Tell the children they are going to have snacks that rhyme with "nickel." Ask the children to try to think of rhymes for nickel. There are a few: tickle and pickle.
2. Explain that the children will be taste-testing several types of pickles to choose their favorite. Give each child a piece of each type of pickle.
3. Let the children share their favorite types of pickles.

Options:
• Graph the children's pickle responses.
• Read the children the Shel Silverstein poem, "Ickle Me, Pickle Me, Tickle Me Too" from *Where the Sidewalk Ends* (Harper & Row, 1974).

Nickels & Dimes

Let's Sing: Nickel & Dime Songs

I Had a Shiny Dime
(to the tune of "The Farmer in the Dell")

I had a shiny dime,
I had a shiny dime,
I put it in my piggy bank,
To spend another time.

Save, Save, Save Your Coins
(to the tune of "Row, Row, Row Your Boat")

Save, save, save your coins,
For a rainy day.
Piggy bank, piggy bank, piggy bank, piggy bank
Keeps them safe today.

This Old Man
(to the tune of "Knick-Knack-Paddywack")

This old man
Had a dime,
He could spend it anytime,
With a knick-knack-paddywack,
This man had a dime.
He could spend it anytime.

Nickels & Dimes

Let's Learn: Mother Goose Rhymes

One for the Money

One to make ready,
And two to prepare;
Good luck to the rider,
And away goes the mare.

One for the money,
Two for the show,
Three to make ready,
And four to go.

Little Miss, Pretty Miss

Little miss, pretty miss,
Blessings light upon you!
If I had half a crown a day,
I'd spend it all upon you.

Note: Half a crown was a British form of money.

"I'm a Nickel!"

"I'm a Dime!"

Quarters

Introduction

• Let's Read:
Lilly's Purple Plastic Purse by Kevin Henkes (Greenwillow, 1996).
Lilly adores her new purple plastic purse, her fancy sunglasses, and her three shiny quarters. She loves them so much, she can't keep quiet about them. When Mr. Slinger, her teacher, holds onto the gifts until the end of the day, Lilly gets angry. Luckily, Lilly and Mr. Slinger are able to work out their differences.

• Let's Talk:
Lilly couldn't wait until show-and-tell to show off her new gifts from Grandma. Discuss a time when the children couldn't wait to do something. Maybe it was waiting for a birthday party, for a grandparent's visit, or for Santa Claus. Have the children share a time when it was difficult to wait.

     This story also provides a good time to discuss anger. Although Lilly is angry at Mr. Slinger, the two still like each other and are able to be friends. Remind the children that it isn't bad to be angry sometimes, then let them share how they deal with their emotions when they are angry.

• Let's Learn:
The quarter features a picture of our first president, George Washington, who served two terms. The back of most quarters has a picture of an eagle, arrows, and an olive branch. In 1976, quarters were made with special pictures featuring America's bicentennial, or 200th birthday. George Washington lived from 1732 to 1799. He was born in Virginia. His picture is also on the one-dollar bill.

Quarters

Let's Create: A Purple Purse

The children will enjoy making purses, or wallets, like Lilly's from *Lilly's Purple Plastic Purse*.

What You Need:

Purple construction paper, tape, stickers, rubber stamps and stamp pads

What You Do:

1. Give each child a sheet of purple construction paper.
2. Demonstrate how to fold the paper into thirds (as shown).
3. Have the children seal two sides of the paper with tape.
4. The children can then fold the top portion of the purse over to keep it closed.
5. The children can decorate their purses with stickers and rubber stamps.

Options:

• Provide colored construction paper for the children to use to make play money to store in their wallets.
• Provide paper clips for the children to use to keep their purses closed. One paper clip on each side will do the job.

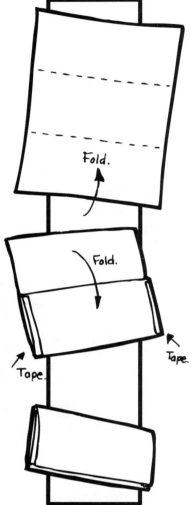

Quarters

Let's Create: Creating a Quilt

Quilt-making is an old-fashioned art. If possible, bring in a patchwork quilt for the children to observe prior to this activity. Consider making a money-themed quilt. Have the children draw pictures of coins or dollars on their squares.

What You Need:

Construction paper or tagboard (in a wide variety of colors), scissors, glue, hole punch, crayons and markers, colored yarn, decorative items (such as sequins, buttons, lace scraps, pictures cut from magazines)

What You Do:

1. Cut the construction paper into squares. Cut one square for each child.
2. Give each child a square of paper to decorate with sequins, buttons, lace scraps, and crayons and markers.
3. Write each child's name on his or her square.
4. Punch holes on all sides of the squares.
5. Lay out a quilt by placing the squares in rows. You might make five rows of five squares each. If your rows do not come out even, have a few children make extra squares. Or mix some undecorated squares into the quilt.
6. Attach the squares by tying pieces of yarn through the holes in the squares.
7. Hang the finished quilt in the classroom.

Book Links:

• *The Patchwork Quilt* by Valerie Flournoy, illustrated by Jerry Pinkney (Dial, 1985).
This is a Reading Rainbow Book.
• *A Name on the Quilt: A Story of Remembrance* by Jeannine Atkins, illustrated by Tad Hills, with photos of panels from the AIDS memorial quilt (Atheneum, 1999).

Quarters

Let's Find Out: Exploring Eagles

The back of most quarters features an eagle, America's national emblem.

What You Need:
Eagle (p. 37), books about eagles (see below), quarters (several for the children to observe), decorative items (buttons, beads, beans, sequins), glue, heavy paper, scissors

What You Do:
1. Duplicate a copy of the bald eagle for each child.
2. Show the children pictures of eagles from books.
3. Explain that the eagle is an important symbol in America. It is featured on the backs of dollar bills, quarters, and fifty-cent pieces. Let the children observe the eagle on the back of the quarters. (Quarters from the bicentennial feature a different design on the back.)
4. Give each child an eagle pattern to glue onto a piece of heavy construction paper.
5. Provide beans, buttons, sequins, and other small decorative items for the children to use to make mosaics. They put a drop of glue where they want to place an item, and then stick the item to the picture.
6. Post the completed mosaics on an "Exciting Eagles" bulletin board. Set various books about eagles on a table near the bulletin board where viewers can look at them.

Book Links:
• *Eagles* by Joe Van Wormer (Dutton, 1985).
This resource features many black-and-white photographs.
• *Eagles of America* by Dorothy Hinshaw Patent, photographs by William Muñoz (Holiday House, 1995).
The color photographs in this book are perfect to share with the children.

Eagle

Quarters

Let's Find Out: Making Change

Early Spanish coins were called "pieces of eight." The coins could be cut into smaller pieces to make change. These pieces were called "bits." Now, people can make change without cutting up their coins.

What You Need:
"I'm a Quarter!" (p. 44), "I'm a Dime!" (p. 32), "I'm a Nickel!" (p. 31), "I'm a Penny!" (p. 19), scissors, large envelope

What You Do:
1. Duplicate one copy of the quarter pattern, two copies of the dime pattern, five copies of the nickel pattern, and 25 of the penny pattern. Cut out the patterns.
2. Gather the children into a circle.
3. Hold up the quarter pattern and have the children tell you how much a quarter is worth. If they don't know, explain that a quarter is worth 25 cents.
4. Spread the other patterns on the floor.
5. Have the children work to see how many different ways they can use the patterns to equal a quarter. They may come up with some of the ways listed below. Help children if they need it.
6. Store all of the patterns in a large envelope for the children to count with during free time.

Ways to Equal a Quarter:
Two dimes and one nickel
Two dimes and five pennies
One dime and three nickels
One dime, two nickels, and five pennies
One dime, one nickel, and ten pennies
One dime and fifteen pennies
Five nickels
Four nickels and five pennies
Three nickels and ten pennies
Two nickels and 15 pennies
One nickel and 20 pennies
25 pennies

Book Link:
• *Jelly Beans for Sale* by Bruce McMillan (Scholastic, 1996). This book shows how different combinations of coins can buy different amounts of jelly beans.

Quarters

Let's Find Out: "Q" Words

What You Need:
Q-Cards (p. 40), paper, crayons or markers, hole punch, brads

What You Do:
1. Duplicate the Q-cards and cut them out.
2. Have the children share as many different words that start with "q" as they can. If the children get stuck, hold up the Q-cards and have them try to name the item on each card.
3. Give each child a sheet of paper.
4. Have each child choose a word that starts with "q" to illustrate.
5. When the pictures are finished, bind them in a "Quite Quirky Q-book."

Option:
• Throughout the year, make alliteration books for each letter of the alphabet.

Book Link:
• *Quiet, Wyatt* by Bill Maynard, illustrated by Frank Remkiewicz (Putnam, 1997).
Wyatt is too little to "dry it," "fry it," or "buy it." However, when he saves the day, people stop telling him to "be quiet, Wyatt."

Q-Cards

quack

quail

quarter

quarterback

queen

question mark

quiet

quill

quilt

Quarters

Let's Play: Q-Card Match-Up
This game is played like "Concentration."

What You Need:
Q-Cards (p. 40), markers or crayons, scissors, clear contact paper or laminator (optional)

What You Do:
1. Duplicate the cards twice, color, and cut out. Laminate or cover with clear contact paper, if desired. Cut out again leaving a thin laminate border to prevent peeling.
2. Demonstrate how to play "Q-Card Match-Up." The children turn all the cards face down. The first child turns two cards over at a time. If the cards match, the child keeps them and takes another turn. If the cards do not match, the child turns them back over and another child takes a turn.

Quarters

Let's Eat: Quarter Sandwiches

What You Need:
Bread, sandwich fillings (see suggestions below), knife (for adult use only), serving plate, paper plates, napkins

What You Do:
1. Make a variety of sandwiches, such as peanut butter and jelly, cream cheese and cucumber, bologna and mustard, and tuna salad.
2. Cut the sandwiches into quarters and put them on serving plates.
3. Let the children choose four quarter sandwiches for snacks. They can choose all of the same type of sandwich, or try four different types.
4. Discuss the way the sandwiches were cut. Each section is one-quarter of a whole sandwich.

Book Link:
• *Eating Fractions* by Bruce McMillan (Scholastic, 1991).
This book uses photographs to show simple fractions of foods, such as a pizza in quarters.

Quarters

Let's Sing: Quarter Songs

My Purse, It Has Three Quarters
(to the tune of "My Hat, It Has Three Corners")

My purse, it has three quarters,
Three quarters has my purse,
And if it had not three quarters,
It would not be my purse!

I'm an Eagle
(to the tune of "Alouette")

I'm an eagle,
Yes, I am an eagle.
I'm an eagle.
I'm a great big bird.
Eagles' favorite food is fish,
They could eat it in a dish.
In a dish,
In a dish,
They love fish,
They love fish.
Ohhhh,
I'm an eagle,
Yes, I am an eagle.
I'm an eagle.
I'm a great, big bird.

Note: Pictures of eagles are found on the backs of quarters, dollar bills, and fifty-cent pieces.

"I'm a Quarter"

Dollars

Introduction

• Let's Read:

Bunny Money by Rosemary Wells (Dial, 1997).
Ruby plans to buy Grandma a lovely music box for her birthday. However, Max has different ideas for gifts. After Max's behavior requires a trip to the laundromat, and after eating lunch, Ruby doesn't have enough money for the music box. Luckily, Grandma is just as happy with the musical earrings from Ruby and the fake vampire teeth from Max. At the end of this book are instructions for making "bunny money."

• Let's Talk:

Ruby saves up her money to buy Grandma a gift. Have the children think about who they would most like to give a present to and what that present would be. The children can share their ideas. Although Ruby is unable to buy Grandma a music box, Grandma is very pleased with the presents from Max and Ruby. Ask the children to remember the favorite present they've received. The children can draw pictures of their favorite presents to share with the class.

• Let's Learn:

The man on the front of the one-dollar bill is George Washington, America's first president, the same man who is featured on the quarter. On the back of the dollar bill is the Great Seal of the United States. The seal features the "Eagle of Democracy." The reverse of the seal, which also appears on the dollar, shows an Egyptian pyramid. The dollar has been the same size since 1929.

Dollars

Let's Create: Funny Money

In *Bunny Money*, the bills feature pictures of bunnies. In this activity, the children will choose their favorite characters, friends, or family to feature on dollar bills.

What You Need:
Colored construction paper, scissors, crayons or markers, Purple Purses (p. 34)

What You Do:
1. Cut the construction paper into dollar-bill sized rectangles.
2. Give several bills to each child.
3. Explain that the children will be making their own money.
4. Have the children brainstorm cartoon characters, characters from children's books, friends, or family that they would like to feature on their money.
5. Provide crayons or markers for the children to use to draw pictures on the bills.
6. Let the children make assorted denominations of bills. They can make all of the bills equal one dollar. Or they can make million-dollar bills, three-dollar bills, and so on.
7. The children can store their Funny Money in their Purple Purses.

Dollars

Let's Create: Pretend Pyramids

On the backs of dollar bills is a picture of an Egyptian pyramid. The pyramid symbolizes "strength."

What You Need:
Back of a bill (see below), colored clay or playdough

What You Do:
1. Show the children a dollar bill, or the drawing of the backside of a dollar. (If you use the pattern, duplicate several for the children to observe up close.)
2. Discuss the different symbols that appear on the back of dollar bills. Have the children name the items they recognize (eagle, shield, branch, feathers, arrows). If none of the children recognizes the pyramid, point out the pyramid. If possible, show the children pictures of pyramids from books.
3. Explain that the children will be making clay pyramids. Give each child a piece of clay to work into a pyramid.
4. Have the children make as many different pyramids as they want out of the different colors of clay.
5. Display the completed pyramids on a table. Place books about pyramids nearby.

Book Link:
• *Pyramid* by James Putnam, photographed by Geoff Brightling & Peter Hayman (Knopf, 1994).
This book discusses Egyptian pyramids and also shows modern pyramids, such as the one at the Louvre in Paris.

Dollars

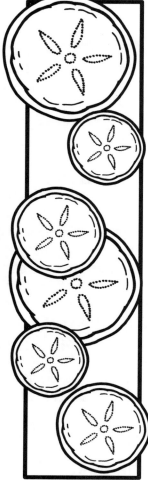

Let's Find Out: Sorting Sand Dollars
Not all dollars are types of money. Sand dollars live in the oceans near the shores. Their round, flat shapes resemble silver dollars.

What You Need:
Super Sand Dollars (p. 49), heavy paper, glitter and glue (in squeeze bottles), scissors, markers

What You Do:
1. Duplicate the Super Sand Dollars onto heavy paper and cut them out. Make one set for each child.
2. Provide glitter and glue in squeeze bottles for the children to use to trace the designs on the sand dollars.
3. Write each child's name on the back of his or her sand dollars. Older children may be able to do this themselves.
4. Once the sand dollars dry, gather them together. Have the children sit in a circle on the floor.
5. Tell the children that they will be sorting the sand dollars by size. Then pick up one of the sand dollars and say, "This is a large sand dollar." Let the children take turns picking up the sand dollars and placing them in the appropriate piles.
6. Make sure each of the children has a chance to sort.

Super Sand Dollars

Dollars

Let's Find Out: A Ten O'Clock Scholar
This is a fun and simple time-telling activity. Make sure to create a clock for yourself.

What You Need:
Clock (p. 51), scissors, brads, crayons or markers, glue

What You Do:
1. Duplicate a copy of the Clock for each child and punch a hole in the center of each Clock.
2. Help the children cut out the clock hands.
3. Demonstrate how to attach the clock hands to the Clock using a brad. (The brad should close in the back.)
4. Let the children decorate their clock faces using crayons or markers.
5. Teach the children the Mother Goose rhyme "A Diller, a Dollar" (p. 61).
6. Put both clock hands at 12 o'clock and hold the clock up. Have the children set their clocks to the same time. Then ask the children what time it is. Lead them through several other time-telling activities, including ten o'clock.
7. The children can continue to practice their time-telling skills.

Clock

12
11
1
10
2
9 O 3
8 4
7 5
6

Dollars

Let's Find Out: King's Countinghouse

In the Mother Goose Rhyme "Sing a Song of Sixpence" (p. 61), the king counts his money in a countinghouse. Teach the children this rhyme before doing the activity.

What You Need:
Royal Money (p. 53), scissors, crayons or markers

What You Do:
1. Duplicate a copy of the Royal Money pattern for each child.
2. Provide crayons and markers for the children to use to decorate their bills.
3. Have the children cut out the royal money. Each child should have ten bills.
4. As a class, work through several simple addition and subtraction problems. For example, have the children take three of their bills and then add two more. Then have the children pretend to be kings and queens counting their money to find the answer.
5. Let the children make up their own simple addition and subtraction problems. One child tells the children how many bills to start with and then how many to take away or add to the pile. The children then count their bills to find the answers.

Options:
• Substitute Monopoly money, or other fake money with numerals, for this activity.
• Do this activity with play coins of different denominations.

Royal Money

Dollars

Let's Find Out: Blackbird Pie

This counting activity is "for the birds."

What You Need:
Blackbirds (p. 55), scissors, pie tin, yarn, 24 clothespins

What You Do:
1. Duplicate the Blackbirds onto black construction paper and cut them out. Make 24 birds.
2. Put the birds in the pie tin.
3. Teach the children the Mother Goose Rhyme "Sing a Song of Sixpence" (p. 61).
4. Bring out the pie tin. Let each child take one blackbird out of the pie. The children should count the birds as they take them out. For example, the first child would say, "One bird," the second would say, "two birds," and line up the second bird next to the first. If the children forget which number they are on, they can count the other birds in the line.
5. When all of the blackbirds have been counted, string a piece of yarn across the classroom. Let the children each clip a bird to the yarn.

Note:
The reference of four-and-twenty in the poem is an old-fashioned way of saying 24.

Blackbirds

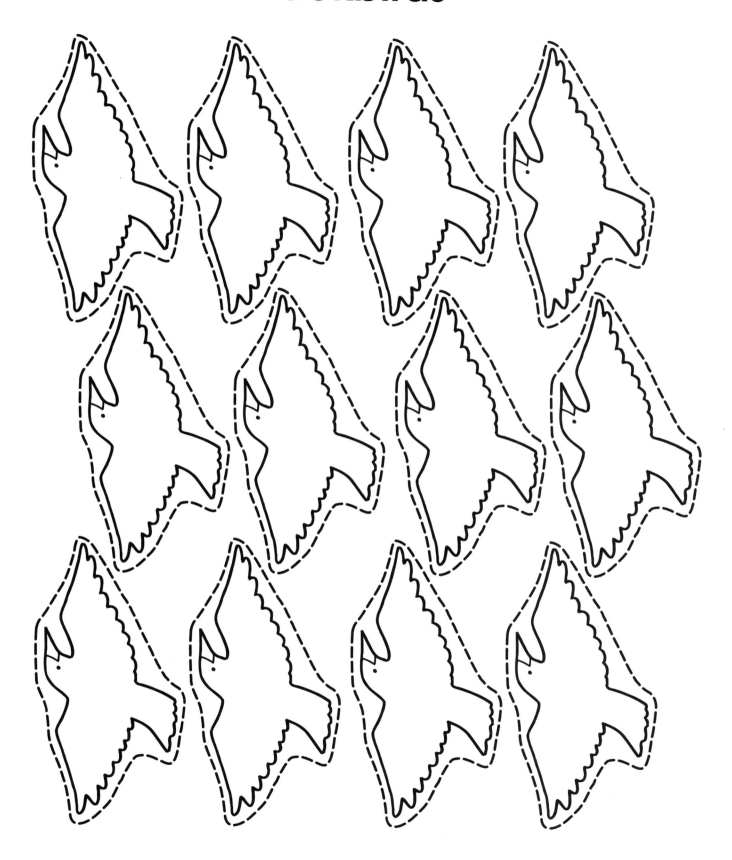

Dollars

Let's Play: Find the Countinghouse

The children will each be trying to reach the king's countinghouse to count the money.

What You Need:
Markers & Spinner (p. 57), Game Board pattern (p. 58), crayons or markers, clear contact paper (or laminating machine), scissors, hole punch, brad

What You Do:
1. Duplicate the Game Board pattern, color, and cover with contact paper. (Or use a laminating machine.)
2. Duplicate the Markers & Spinner, cut out, color, cover with clear contact paper, and cut out again. (Leave a thin laminate border to help prevent peeling.)
3. Punch a hole in the center of the spinner, and attach the arrow using the brad.
4. Explain the game. Three children may play at a time. The players are each little blackbirds trying to get to the king's countinghouse first. The first child to land at the spot marked "finish" is the winner.

Markers & Spinner

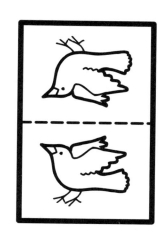
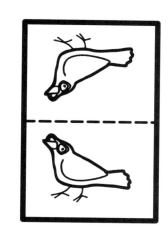

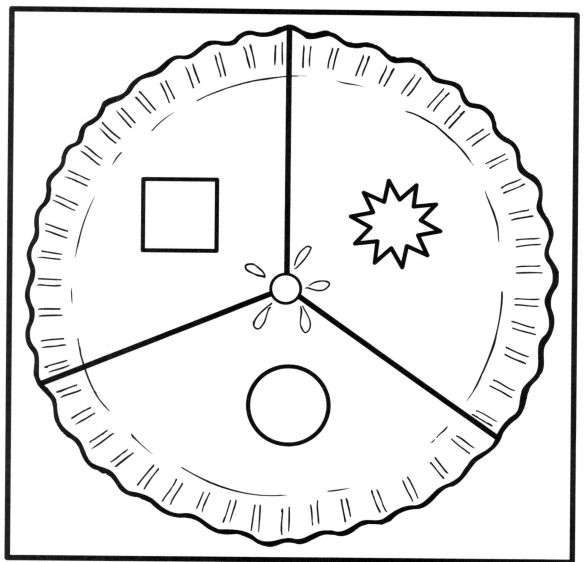

Game Board

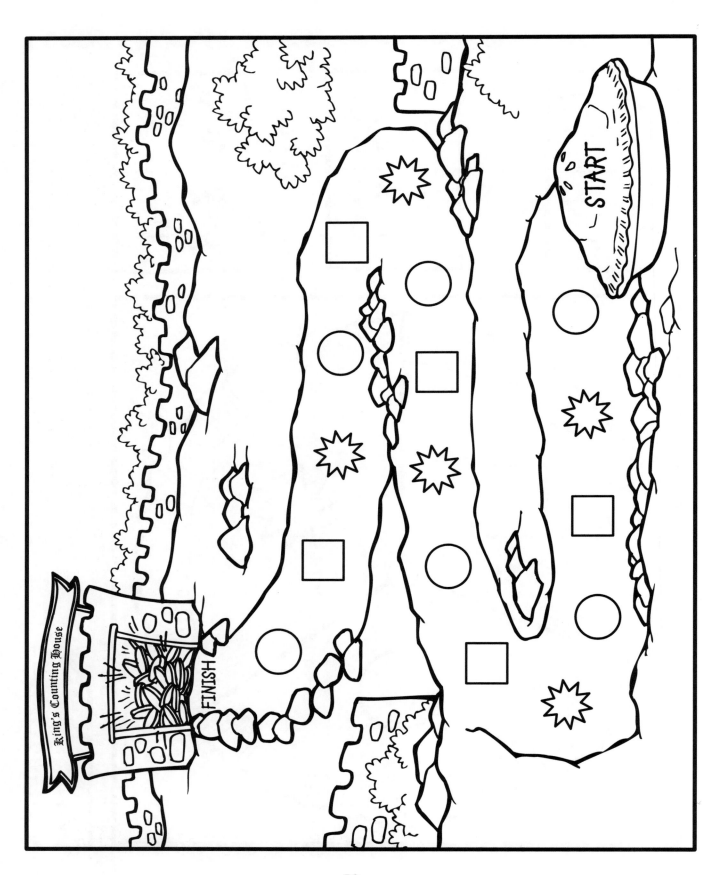

START

FINISH

King's Counting House

Dollars

Let's Eat: Bread and Honey

What You Need:
Bread, honey, plastic knives, paper plates, napkins

What You Do:
1. Teach the children the Mother Goose Rhyme "Sing a Song of Sixpence" (p. 61).
2. Serve a snack of bread and honey, which is what the queen snacked on while the king was counting money.

Option:
• Have a taste test of different types or flavors of honey. Have the children spread a bit of each different type on bread. Ask the children to choose their favorite type. Graph the results.

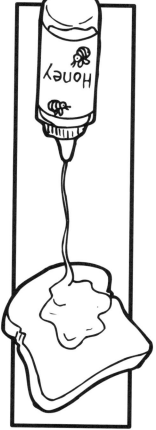

Dollars

Let's Sing: Dollar Songs

I Am a Dollar
(to the tune of "You Are My Sunshine")

I am a dollar,
A bright green dollar.
I'm worth four quarters.
I'm worth ten dimes.
I travel often,
When someone spends me,
But I'm in pockets
Most of the time.

I'm a Little Dollar
(to the tune of "I'm a Little Teapot")

I'm a little dollar,
I'm worth one.
On my face is Washington.
I'm a mix of colors, green and black,
And there's an eagle on my back.

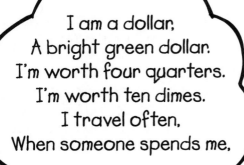

I am a dollar,
A bright green dollar.
I'm worth four quarters.
I'm worth ten dimes.
I travel often,
When someone spends me,

Dollars

Let's Learn: Mother Goose Rhymes

A Diller, a Dollar

A diller, a dollar,
A ten o'clock scholar,
What makes you come so soon?
You used to come at ten o'clock,
And now you come at noon.

Sing a Song of Sixpence

Sing a song of sixpence,
A pocket full of rye;
Four-and-twenty blackbirds
Baked in a pie.

When the pie was opened,
The birds began to sing;
Wasn't that a dainty dish
To set before the king?

The king was in his counting-house
Counting out his money;
The queen was in the parlor
Eating bread and honey.

The maid was in the garden
Hanging out the clothes,
Along came a blackbird
And nipped off her nose.

Note: A sixpence was a British type of money.

"I'm a Dollar!"

Gold & Silver

Introduction

• Let's Read:
Rumpelstiltskin retold and illustrated by Paul Galdone (Clarion, 1985).
A miller brags to the king that his lovely daughter can spin straw into gold. The king puts the daughter to a test—if she cannot spin straw into gold she will die. A little man appears to help the daughter. The price of his help is her first-born child. When the time comes to collect the child, the daughter doesn't want to give up her baby. The little man says that he will forgo the debt if she can guess his name. With help from a faithful servant, she does. Another version of this famous tale is retold and illustrated by Paul O. Zelinsky (Dutton, 1986).

• Let's Talk:
The miller tries to impress the king by bragging that his daughter has an amazing skill. Have the children think about a skill that they would most like to have. It could be something magical, such as spinning straw into gold or flying on a spaceship. Or it could be something more tangible, such as riding a two-wheeler without training wheels or learning how to play a musical instrument.

• Let's Learn:
Early in history, people did not have money. Instead, people traded goods and services. The first metal money was invented by Sumerians who were the first to melt silver into small bars. Each bar was stamped with the exact weight to tell people how much silver they were getting or giving in return for goods or services. Gold has also been used for money.

Gold & Silver

Let's Create: Treasure Chests

The king in *Rumpelstiltskin* is rich, but he wants to be richer still. In this activity, the children will draw pictures of things that are precious to them.

What You Need:
Treasure Chest (p. 65), crayons or markers, glitter mixed with glue (in squeeze bottles), hole punch and yarn or brads (if making a book)

What You Do:
1. Discuss the story *Rumpelstiltskin*. In the story, the king was already wealthy, but his greed makes him want even more. In order for Rumpelstiltskin to help her, the miller's daughter promises him her first-born child. But the child turns out to be more precious to her than any amount of gold or silver.
2. Have the children think about the most precious things that they have. These things could be actual objects, such as a bicycle, or the items could be their family members, their friends, and so on.
3. Duplicate a copy of the Treasure Chest for each child. Have the children draw pictures of their most precious items inside the chests. Glitter mixed with glue will add extra sparkle to the pictures.
4. The children can each dictate a sentence about their precious items.
5. Post the completed pictures in the classroom.

Treasure Chest

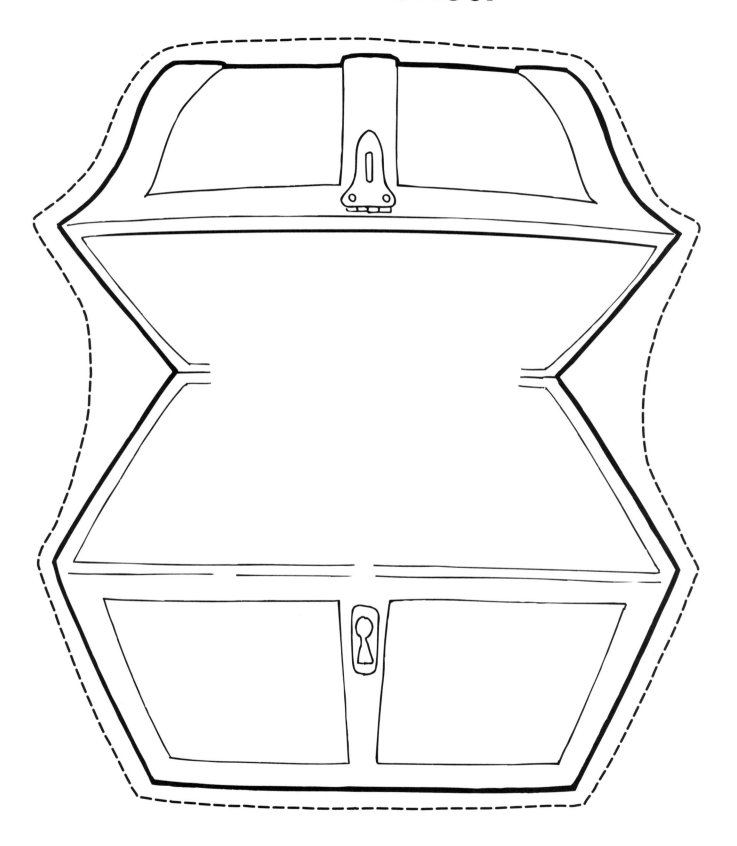

Gold & Silver

Let's Create: The Midas Touch
There are a variety of fables about gold. The king with the Midas touch is one famous tale.

What You Need:
Gold or yellow tempera paint, paintbrushes, shallow pans (for paint)

What You Do:
1. Read or tell the children the story of King Midas.
2. Explain that the children will be pretending to be King (or Queen) Midas.
3. Give each child a sheet of paper.
4. Have the children imagine that they have the Midas touch. Everything they touch turns to gold. The children can then pretend to be at their house, or in their rooms. They should draw a picture using only the gold paint to show what has happened to all the different objects they've touched.
5. Ask the children whether or not they would like to have the Midas touch and why or why not.
6. Post the paintings on a "Glittering Gold" bulletin board.

Options:
• Throughout the year, have the children make other paintings or pictures using only one color. Keep the paintings to post in a final art show—chronicling the children's "blue periods," "red periods," "gold periods," and so on.
• Show the children pictures by famous artists who focused on using only one color, or very few colors, of paint.

Gold & Silver

Let's Find Out: What's in a Name?

In the fable *Rumpelstiltskin*, the miller's daughter must guess the little man's name in order to save her baby. His name was very important to the daughter.

What You Need:
Baby name books, crayons or markers, paper, hole punch, yarn or brads

What You Do:
1. Ahead of time, look up the children's names in the baby books and write down the meanings.
2. Gather the children in a circle. Explain that some names have meanings. For example, the name Anna means grace.
3. Have the children brainstorm what they would each like their names to mean.
4. Provide paper and crayons or markers for the children to use to draw pictures of what they would like their names to mean, or what their names mean to them.
5. Tell the children what the books say that their names mean. The children can compare the book's definitions of their names to their own choices.
6. Bind the completed pictures in a "What's in a Name?" book.

Note: If you can't find a name in one of the baby books, consider contacting the parents to ask if they know the meaning behind their child's name, or if their child's name has a special meaning to them.

Gold & Silver

Let's Find Out: Panning for Gold

When gold was discovered in California in 1848, miners in camps used gold dust and nuggets as money. Gold dust was also used as money in Australia.

What You Need:

Rocks or pebbles, gold spray paint, sand table, water, sieves, newsprint

What You Do:

1. Spray paint the rocks or pebbles gold. Do this when the children are not present. Let the "gold nuggets" dry on newsprint.
2. Make a watery mixture of sand and water at the sand table. Set out sieves. Bury the "gold nuggets" in the sand.
3. Discuss the concept of mining for gold. When gold was discovered in California, there was a rush (the gold rush) of miners who came to strike their fortunes. These people used sieves to strain gold dust and nuggets from streams where gold was found.
4. Let the children use the sieves and additional water to pan for gold at the sand table. (Children will have to take turns doing this activity.)
5. After each child sifts sand, the nuggets should be reburied in the sand.

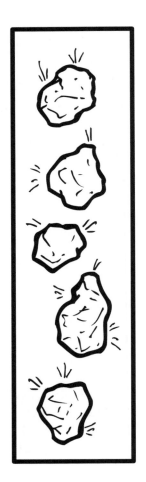

Gold & Silver

Let's Find Out: Other Words for Money

What You Need:
Books about money (see **Nonfiction Resources**), drawing paper, crayons or markers

What You Do:
1. Explain to the children that in other parts of the world, people have different types of money. See the list below for different types of money. Have the children practice saying these different words.
2. Have the children picture different types of American money. Show pictures in books. Have the children brainstorm words that describe money. Lead the discussion, in case children have a difficult time. Prompt the children by suggesting that money could be called something else based on its color (green for bills, silver and copper or brown for coins), or for its size, or for the way it feels, or the pictures on it.
3. Give each child a piece of paper.
4. Have the children draw pictures of money.
5. Let each child have a turn dictating a word or a descriptive phrase for his or her money.
6. Post the finished pictures on a bulletin board that lists the different foreign currencies.

Note:
If any of the children in your class speak other languages, have them share their country's word for money.

Money in Other Countries:
Brazil: New Curzado
Canada: Dollar
China: Yuan
Ecuador: Sucre
Ethiopia: Birr
Greece: Drachma
India: Rupee
Israel: Shekel
Italy: Lira
Japan: Yen
Saudi Arabia: Riyal
Zambia: Kwacha

Gold & Silver

Let's Play: Midas Touch Tag

Play this game outside on a sunny day.

What You Need:
King Midas fable

What You Do:
1. Tell the children the story of King Midas, or read a version of this famous fable.
2. Explain that the children will be playing tag. One child will be "it." This child will have the "Midas touch." When this child tags another child, the tagged child must stay frozen. Play continues until all of the children are tagged. The last child to be tagged becomes the next King Midas. (When girls are "it," they can be Queen Midas.)

Gold & Silver

Let's Play: Catch the Golden Goose

In this game, the children each try to be the first to reach the goose that lays the golden eggs.

What You Need:

Markers & Spinner (p. 72), Game Board pattern (p. 73), crayons or markers, clear contact paper (or laminating machine), scissors, hole punch, brad

What You Do:

1. Duplicate the Game Board pattern, color, and cover with contact paper. (Or use a laminating machine.)
2. Duplicate the Markers & Spinner, cut out, color, cover with clear contact paper, and cut out again. (Leave a thin laminate border to help prevent peeling.)
3. Punch a hole in the center of the spinner, and attach the arrow using the brad.
4. Explain the game. Three children may play at a time. The players are each farmers trying to be the first to reach the golden goose. The first child to land at the spot marked "finish" is the winner.

Markers & Spinner

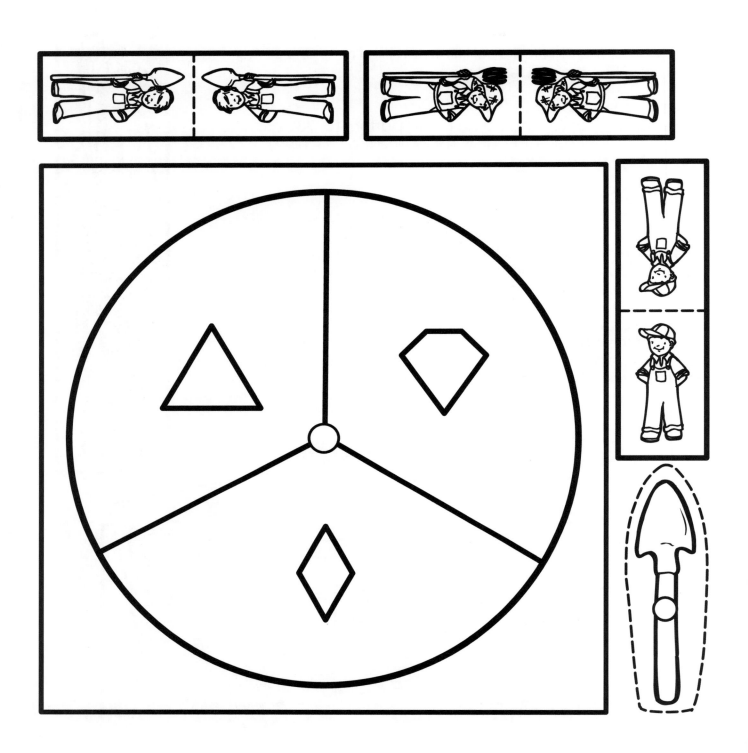

Game Board

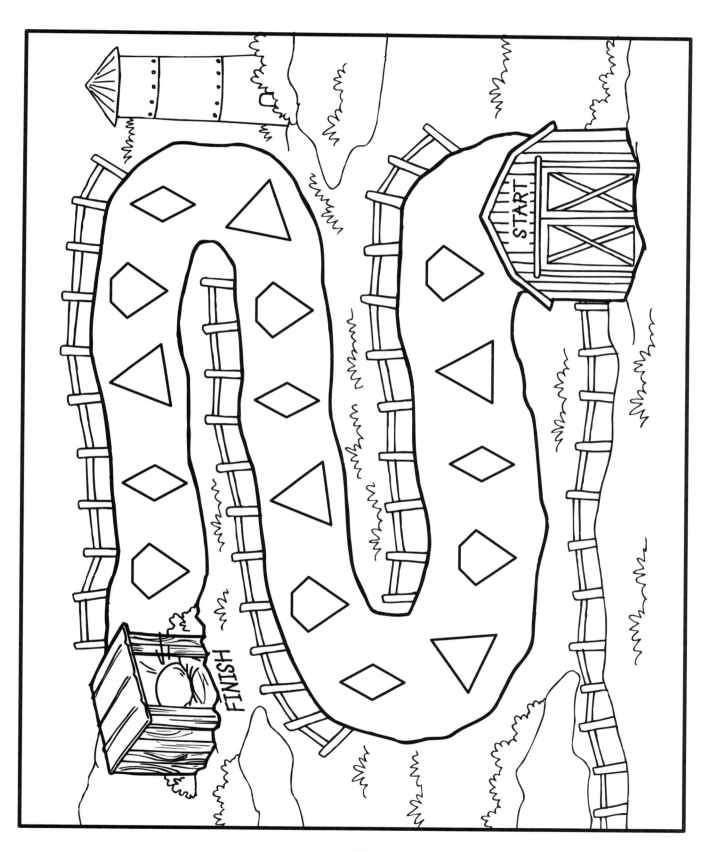

73

Gold & Silver

Let's Eat: Golden Egg Snacks

Read a version of "The Goose That Laid the Golden Egg," or tell the children this story before making this snack.

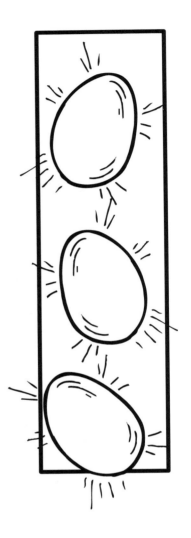

What You Need:
Hard-boiled eggs (one per child), egg-dyeing kit (available before Easter) or yellow food coloring, crackers, salt and pepper, mayonnaise (optional), chopped parsley (optional), plastic utensils, paper plates, napkins

What You Do:
1. Set up egg-dyeing stations according to the directions on the kit. Make several stations to speed up the process.
2. Explain that the children will be making "golden" eggs, like the ones in the story.
3. Demonstrate how to dye the eggs yellow.
4. Help the children make golden egg snacks once the eggs are dry. They peel off the shells, and either cut the eggs into slices to serve on crackers, or make egg salad by mixing in mayonnaise, salt and pepper, and parsley.
5. The children can pretend to be eating real gold eggs as they snack on their golden eggs.

Other "Golden" Snacks to Serve:
• Golden-hued pears—teach the children the Mother Goose rhyme "I Had a Little Nut Tree" (p. 76)— bananas, Ritz crackers, Golden Delicious apples, yellow jelly beans.

Gold & Silver

Let's Sing: Gold & Silver Songs

If You Had Some Gold
(to the tune of "Do Your Ears Hang Low?")

If you had some gold,
Would you save it 'til you're old?
Would you put it in a bank?
Would you listen to it clank?
Would you go out to the store
Spend it now or save some more?
If you had some gold.

I'm a Pretty Gold Coin
(to the tune of "I'm a Little Teapot")

I'm a pretty gold coin
Shining bright,
Watch me sparkle in the light.
Save me for a rainy day,
Or spend me on some fun today.

Another gold-related song to sing:
• Clementine (about a miner/49er).

I'm a pretty gold coin
Shining bright,
Watch me sparkle in the light.

Gold & Silver

Let's Learn: Mother Goose Rhymes

Mary, Mary, Quite Contrary

Mary, Mary, quite contrary,
How does your garden grow?
With silver bells and cockleshells,
And pretty maids all in a row.

I Had a Little Nut Tree

I had a little nut tree,
Nothing would it bear
But a silver nutmeg
And a golden pear.

London Bridge

London Bridge is broken down,
Broken down, broken down,
London Bridge is broken down,
My fair lady.

Build it up with silver and gold,
Silver and gold, silver and gold,
Build it up with silver and gold,
My fair lady.

In Marble Halls

In marble halls as white as milk,
Lined with a skin as soft as silk,
Within a fountain crystal-clear,
A golden apple doth appear.
No doors there are to this stronghold,
Yet thieves break in and steal the gold.

(The answer to this riddle is an egg.)

"We're Gold & Silver"

Storybook Resources

• *Bunny Money* by Rosemary Wells (Dial, 1997).
Max and Ruby have different ideas about what Grandma might like for her birthday.

• *The Go-Around Dollar* by Barbara Johnston Adams, illustrated by Joyce Audy Zarins (Four Winds Press, 1992). When a dollar falls out of someone's pocket, it takes a long journey.

• *Max's Dragon Shirt* by Rosemary Wells (Dial, 1991).
Max and Ruby have five dollars to buy Max a new pair of pants, but what Max really wants is a dragon shirt. And somehow, he manages to get it.

• *Pigs Will Be Pigs* by Amy Axelrod, illustrated by Sharon McGinley-Nally (Four Winds Press, 1994).
When a hungry family of pigs wants to go out to dinner, they search the house for spare change.

• *Rumpelstiltskin* retold and illustrated by Paul Galdone (Clarion, 1985).
A miller brags to the king that his lovely daughter can spin straw into gold.

Nonfiction Resources

Buffalo Books:
• *The American Bison* by Steve Potts, photographs by William Munoz and Lynn Stone (Capstone, 1997).
• *Back from the Edge: The American Bison* by Lynn M. Stone (Rourke, 1991).
• *Return of the Buffalo* by Jack Denton Scott, photographs by Ozzie Sweet (Putnam's Sons, 1976).

Money Books:
• *Money* by Joe Cribb (Knopf, 1990).
• *Money, Money, Money* by Nancy Winslow Parker (HarperCollins, 1995).
• *The Story of Money* by Betsy Maestro, illustrated by Giulio Maestro (Clarion, 1993).

Pyramid Books:
• *Ancient Egypt* by Rosalie and Antony E. David, illustrated by David Salariya and Shirley Willis (Warwick, 1984).
• *Exploring Ancient Egypt* by John Malam (Evans Brothers, 1997).
• *Pyramid* by James Putnam (Knopf, 1994).

Nonfiction Resources

Money Web Sites:

http://www.usmint.gov/default.htm
This is the United States Mint's main Web page.

http://www.usmint.gov/dollarcoin/
This page features a picture of a Susan B. Anthony coin
as well as the latest coin commemorating Sacagawea,
who assisted in the Lewis and Clark expedition.

http://www.usmint.gov/50states/index.cfm
This page features information about the five new quarters
that will be issued each year from 1999 through 2008. It gives
information for submitting a design for your state.

Play Money:
Packages of play U.S. coins and U.S. currency
are available at teacher supply stores, as well as
some office supply stores.

Money Stickers:
Stickers featuring U.S. money (bills and coins)
are available from Mrs. Grossman's.